It's Just Not That Complicated

—————————————————————————————————

It's Just Not That Complicated

A Collection of Stories Revealing the Fingerprints
Of the Creator in Everyday Life

John F Hodgson

Crooked Creek Press
2019

ISBN 978-1-79481-286-4

Crooked Creek Press,
a division of Bigfoot Strategies, LLC
Fisherville, KY

Dedication

To my beautiful wife Robin, who makes me happy in the little things of everyday life, and keeps the home fires burning to enable me to pursue my adventures… and drives me to the E.R. when things go awry.

Contents

Acknowledgements

I must acknowledge the unwitting participants in the experiences that led to writing of this book – my wife, my children, a barnyard full of funny critters, a few family members, and a few friends and neighbors. Thanks for laughing with me, (or at me), as appropriate.

Introduction

I have always thrived on being connected to nature. I relish the feel of warm garden soil on my bare feet in the spring, the smell of fresh cut grass in the summer, the visual feast of fall colors, and the sounds of utter peace as snow falls on a glade of evergreens. My father was a great observer of the ordinary: he could sit for hours watching faces in a crowd, ants working, or a bird building a nest - and be perfectly content. My mother always had the need to write about that which she felt and experienced. That love of observation was passed on to me, along with the need to write about it.

Over the years, I have gradually become aware that the Creator is talking to us all the time. He does not shout, but instead quietly uses the subtlety of his Creation to illustrate his character. He uses everyday situations to instruct us in his truth. The Bible says that he inhabits the praise of his people, and I think he must also laugh with us, at the situations we humans get ourselves into. I seem to get into a lot of them....

This book has no plot, no real beginning or end. It is not meant to be read cover to cover in one sitting, but to be enjoyed a story at a time when you have a moment to relax, to laugh, and to reflect on the life that the Creator has placed us in. Most of the stories are about experiences I have lived and laughed through, and I invite you to step into my memories for a moment as you read, and enjoy the view.

The Birds of Spring

1994

Every spring, the birds come to build a nest somewhere around my house. They can be annoying at first, as we negotiate the terms of their seasonal lease. After a week or two of them starting nests and me removing them, we agree that my barbecue grill is a less than optimal location, and they settle for an out of the way eave.

In the spring of 1993, the nest was right in front of our kitchen window in the porch rafters of an old farmhouse we lived in. My wife and I watched the progress of nest building with modest interest until 4 baby birds began chirping. First, we were amused, then irritated at their incessant chatter. My wife swears that their cries of hunger were synchronized with those of our 2-month-old son, adding more stress to her life.

Gradually, however, they won us both over. Their little beaks had white outlines that looked just like four tiny clowns faces chirping at us out of the dark nest. We came to enjoy watching their growth, and watching mother and father bird in constant shuttle flight to feed them. I think we must have felt a kinship with their "new parent" situation that was so much like our own.

One June night, as I came in the house after a relaxing swing in the hammock, my blood ran cold. A four-foot snake - the very embodiment of evil in my book - had somehow scaled the porch column, and was up in the nest swallowing the last of the baby birds. How could this intruder have come so close to my loved ones without my knowing? And how dare he eat my little friends! My wife wept with empathy for the mother who had worked so hard to feed these little ones. I loaded the shotgun, and dispatched the snake along with a portion of my porch roof. It was worth it. I assume any snake near my house in the dark to be poisonous! (He wasn't, but I gave him a criminal's burial in the yard anyway.)

Thinking Deeper:

As I cleaned up the mess, I pondered how cruel and hard nature can be, and how *violated* I felt that this snake had spoiled our lovely spring evening. I questioned God - Why? Then it hit me - I had just been praying in the hammock for God to help me guard my tongue, and to help me draw closer to Him - everything in my life was fine, but I had been drifting away a bit in complacency.

Just as the loud cries of the birds had drawn the snake to them, my ungodly speech might be drawing Satan to me. Just as they were complacent in their seemingly safe nest, I was complacent in my pleasant and safe life. Just as the snake had devoured them in a moment, Satan prowls about like a roaring lion to devour *me*, if the slip of my tongue gives him opportunity. The Bible is not a shotgun, but it is called a sword - and tonight I was reminded to use it to keep the snake away from *my* nest.

If there are animals in heaven, I will thank my little feathered friends for their message. May God rest their little souls.

The 4th of July

1968

Back in Texas in the 1960s, my family and I enjoyed the simple pleasures of life together. I spent hours in the yard playing with my pet goat BB, playing in an old rubber tire swing, and playing with other "toys" that included an empty 55-gallon barrel to roll on, and a concrete drainage pipe to crawl through. That was normal summer life, killing time and wishing for a trip to the lake to cool off.

The 4th of July was always a very special day at the lake. Mom would start making preparations early in the morning, making delicious summer treats like watermelon balls, deviled eggs and potato salad and packing them into a big cooler.   Dad would pack the car with folding chairs and picnic blankets, and we would all get our swimsuits and a set of dry clothes packed up. It would be a long day at the lake, and we needed to be prepared! Next, we would drive to KFC and get a giant bucket of chicken that would torture me with the intoxicating smell of "the Colonel's secret 11 herbs and spices" for hours until it was time for dinner.

My brother and I could barely contain ourselves 20 miles later when we pulled up to the firework stand. We would both have money saved from summer chores to buy enough fireworks to blow all our fingers off a dozen times. Back in the good old days before the Government Safety Monitors took over, a 7-year old boy could go just across the city limits and get some incredible fireworks that were incredibly dangerous.

When we finally made it to the lake, we would stake out a place with blankets on the wide grassy area by the water. The blanket would serve as "home base" for the kids, as we would run off for swimming, popping fire-crackers and having mud fights in the lake. Mom and dad were perfectly content to sit with a cold drink in the shade and socialize while we ran around.

About once an hour, we would make our way back to "home base" to get a snack or drink, and inquire as to when we might actually be able to eat some of that chicken. Dinner finally came about sundown, and we would eat until our little bellies ached. Along about dark, we would be worn out and stuffed, and the whole family would squeeze in tight on the blanket so we could all see the sky for the firework show. We would 'ooh" and "ahh" and clap, and my sister would scream at the really loud ones.

Finally, around 10 PM, the show would be over, and we would gather our stuff and drag back to the car, literally having had as much fun as we could stand. For the highlight of the day, we got to skip brushing our teeth that night, since the kids would all be virtually unconscious when we got home. I vaguely remember dad dragging me down the hall to my bed where I slept like a brick until July 5th.

Over 40 years later, my siblings and I still fondly remember those times together. Family traditions help kids form strong bonds with each other, and cement memories around the observance of a special day.

Thinking Deeper:

About 3000 years ago, God gave the children of Israel special holidays to observe as well. They would travel to a meeting place, eat a feast together, socialize, play, and remember a special event as directed by God. Their Passover celebration was a little like our Independence Day, as they memorialized being freed from slavery in Egypt by God.

God gave us another celebration tradition when Jesus came to earth, reminiscent of the Passover. The Lord's Supper – Communion - is a celebration of our being set free from sin, and a memorial observance that we can partake of and remember as a family. Now there is something worthy of a celebration!

A Grumpy Christmas

2004

I don't like Christmas very much. Wait…before you get out the torches and pitchforks to run me out of town, let me explain. When I was a kid, we always left town for Christmas to avoid what my mom called the "rat race". Many a year I saw Santa on the chair lift as I was skiing on Christmas Day in Colorado. Getting to ski and enjoy the beautiful mountains was present enough for me. At the lodge, we would decorate a huge pine tree, freshly cut from the mountain, sing a few carols, play some games, and have a nice Christmas dinner. Gifts were small and few, and commercialism was almost non-existent. There were no shopping lines, no piles of cards to address, no pressure, no cheesy decorations. I have many warm, pleasant memories from those Christmases past.

For most of my adult life, I have worked up until late Christmas Eve helping the rest of the world get their gifts on time. Working for the world's largest package delivery company, I have delivered packages, loaded trucks, dug airplanes out of the snow, and have generally been very, very busy from Thanksgiving until Santa starts hitching up the reindeer. Squeezing in shopping, decorating and addressing cards is not something I enjoy after a long day at work. By the time I am ready to relax, the holiday is just about over. My wife has suggested that to avoid psychological damage to our 2 children, I should at least *pretend* that I like decorating the tree and hanging lights. (I don't, but I am learning to fake it better.) My recent memories of Christmas include feeling pressured, overwhelmed, tired, over-commercialized and generally Grinch-like.

One year, just to bring my Christmas pressure to a new level, we moved into a lovely new, self-contracted home that was 99% finished. For some reason, the last 1% took me from August until Christmas to get completed. Doing all the work myself only cost me $20,000 more than hiring a professional, but at least it gave me to something to do every night, weekend and vacation for a year as I neglected my family. Needless to say, by the time Christmas week rolled around, I was less than "jolly".

I am usually not one who looks for visible "signs" from God, but I think he sent me one that year, to help me gain perspective on my house building and Christmas mania. Just before Christmas, the sun came out of the clouds at just the right angle to cast the perfect shadow of a cross on my fireplace mantle. It overshadowed the Christmas stockings hanging there.

Thinking Deeper:

The shadow dominated the exact center of my house at about 3 pm, the time Jesus was crucified. That event overshadows all of creation, overshadows the house that I have created with my hands, overshadows all of our Christmas decorations and traditions. That is what I want my Christmas celebration to center on.

I might just get the Christmas spirit after all.

Of Boys and Forts

1972

As a boy growing up in the 1970s, my friends and I loved to build forts and play army. Every Christmas season, the boys in my neighborhood would look with eager anticipation at our neighbor's Christmas trees. One of the happiest days of the post-Christmas week was the day before trash pick-up. People would simply haul these glorious trees out to the curb for the trash man, only to have them intercepted by a small army of boys on Schwinn Stingray bikes. We would drag the trees off to somebody's backyard and build that most treasured holiday tradition – the "Christmas Tree Fort". A good fort would be 2 tree-lengths wide and 3 tree-layers high. It smelled great inside there, and the walls were springy enough to deflect many of the dirt clods and acorns the attacking army would throw. A good fort could withstand a solid week of siege by the invading army before all the needles fell off.

As I got older, we moved on to more advanced forts made of wood. Lumber was expensive, and my frugal dad would not buy me any brand-new lumber for a fort. Instead, we went way out past the edge of town to a dumpy place that sold "used" lumber from old houses that had been torn down. You could get a board for the low, low price of 10 cents, but most still had nails in them and were covered with old peeling paint. In order to build something, I had to spend hours beating the old nails out of the boards. Some had split ends that had to be sawn off by hand to make them usable, and that 50-year-old lumber was as hard as a rock! Even after you pulled out the nails and sawed the ends square, the lumber still looked very "used"; Dad said it just had "character". Either way, it still made a fort that would withstand dirt clods from the enemy army.

Thinking Deeper:

Thirty-five years later, my kids were helping me "recycle" some old lumber by pulling the nails out. As I told them about my childhood fort building experiences, it occurred to me that Jesus might have had a similar experience. His Dad did not give him much "new lumber" to build his church with. He got old boards, full of nails, dents, cracks and peeling paint. He had to pull out the nails of sin and trim off broken ends of lives. Some boards were barely usable and required special care – but His Dad saw that they had "character" after Jesus fixed them up. Somehow, the Carpenter took this poor material and built his fort – the church – with it, and not only did it resist dirt clod attacks, but according to Matthew 16:18, the very gates of Hell cannot stand against it.

POSTSCRIPT:

Back in the 70's in Fort Worth, one of my best friends was a freckled, red headed kid with a big smile named George. We were schoolmates and teammates for 5 years, but also rode bikes together, took family trips together, ran through the woods, shot BB guns at each other, and even ("accidentally") burned down the "fort" you see pictured with us together (George is on the left) That is a story in itself.

In 7th grade, we even shared some experiences that were the beginnings of our faith in Christ, that would come to shape both our lives and families in the succeeding 40+ years.

We lived our good and busy lives 1000 miles apart, and would occasionally pass messages and hear news about each other through my mother, when she was alive. I missed him, but never could find him on Facebook. I always meant to make time to track him down visit him when I was in Texas, but... never did.

In 2017, George was buried in a plot that would have been visible from the top of our "fort" in 1974, in what used to be the wooded cemetery backlot behind my childhood home, the woods we used to play in. Cancer took him so fast at age 56 there was no time to catch up, or even say goodbye - I did not even know he was sick. By all reports, George lived a great life, and was a beloved family man, businessman, philanthropist and community leader. I like to think he got a chuckle in heaven, knowing that his body was laid to rest so close to the site of our adolescent adventures.

Costa Rica

2008

My friend Larry and I have enjoyed taking a number of "man trips" over the years. We go places that our wives would never want to visit, and do things that our insurance agents would not want to know about. One year the desired destination was the rain forest (read: jungle) in Costa Rica. Larry pointed out that they have beautiful scenery, waterfalls, incredible bird watching, snorkeling, jungle wildlife and many other things to do and see. My wife, a.k.a. The Official Safety Monitor, pointed out that Costa Rica is a 3rd world country, they speak a foreign language there, they have 327 kinds of poisonous snakes, and the jungles are full of insects.

After carefully considering the options, Larry and I decided to go for it. After all, we had rented a car over the Internet, we had a map of the country, and Larry knew the Spanish words to order chicken and rice with a diet Coke. Just to reassure the girls, I packed a first aid kit with all the necessary supplies, and some super strong 98% DEET insect repellant to keep the bugs away. What could be safer?

Upon arrival in San Jose, we picked up our car and set out on the 10-mile drive to our first overnight stop. Four hours later, as darkness and hunger began to descend upon us, we discovered that San Jose has no street signs and no one who can speak enough English to give directions. On a positive note, the local McDonalds serves chicken, rice and diet Coke so we were able to order dinner. I finally resorted to the Universal language, and paid a cabdriver 20 bucks to lead us down a maze of darkened back streets to our hotel. And our wives had worried about us! Ha! It was a great relief to finally have a place to lie down.

As we drifted off to sleep, I began to snore like an outboard engine with a carburetor problem. After repeated complaints from my roommate, I rummaged through my suitcase for my "Snore Relief" spray. I found the bottle by shape in the dark, and squirted 2 doses down my throat... of 98% DEET insect repellant. The only word I was able to choke out was "IDIOT!" as I gagged, retched, and searched for some way to rinse the horrible tasting, burning, suffocating stuff out of my throat.

I threw the bottle at a very startled Larry to read the "in case of swallowing" directions. We suddenly realized we could not do what the label said – there was no cell phone, no poison control center to call, no way to get to a hospital, and no way to explain in Spanish why this idiot Gringo had sprayed insect repellant down his throat. Larry's ability to order chicken and rice in Spanish was no help whatsoever. All I could do was pray, gargle, spit and repeat - a thousand times. The dose I ingested was apparently not fatal, since I lived through the night. My breath was horrible the next day, but then again, no insects came near me for a week either.

Thinking Deeper:

I reached out in the darkness, and thought I had found medicine, when in fact I had found poison that just looked like medicine. This case of mistaken identity could have killed me. When you are in a strange, dark place in your life and are reaching for help, be sure you know what it is that you are taking for spiritual medicine. Make sure that the medicine that you take for your soul is the truth before you swallow it! I think this is what the apostle John meant in 1 John 4:1

" Dear friends, do not believe every spirit, but test the spirits to see whether they are from God, because many false prophets have gone out into the world...".

Lesson learned.

The Cow Lick

(An Experiential Etymology)

1994

At the tender age of 16 months, my son Caleb loved to play outside more than any kid I know. One of his favorite things to do was to go running through our garden, arms flailing, with only a wisp of blonde "cow-lick" visible above the tops of the tomato plants. He paused now and then to pick a ripe tomato, and ate it right there. By the time he finished two or three of them, he was covered with juice, seeds, and dirt from the eyebrows to the knees. He was happy as can be, and my wife Robin, (Official Safety Monitor) was concerned a little about the after effects of all those tomatoes, but usually let him have his fun.

Our nosey neighbor called once to ask Robin if she knew just *where* Caleb was right now, apparently alarmed at his lightly supervised agricultural excursion. Robin, on returning from answering the phone, had to locate Caleb by the sounds of his hysterical laughter. Caleb had stuck his sticky little face through the fence, and our yearling calf Rosebud had just finished licking the last of the tomato juice off his face. Both were delighted with the arrangement. The Official Safety Monitor inspected for damage, but everything looked normal, except for the addition of a sticky new "cow lick" in the *front* of his hair. Some study the origin of strange words in a library, we have found field experience to be much more enjoyable!

La Fortuna

2008

My friend Larry and I had the chance to do an "adventure vacation" in Costa Rica, Central America. It is an absolutely gorgeous land of natural wonders, almost like the Garden of Eden. It has rain forests, waterfalls, majestic mountains, wildlife, and the most colorful birds imaginable.

There are also dangers in this beautiful country. Millions of its inhabitants live within lava-spitting range of several massive volcanoes, and there are poisonous snakes that can kill you before you have time to look up "hospital" in your Spanish-English dictionary.

One quaint little town we visited was called "La Fortuna" – The Fortunate. This town was just beyond the edge of total destruction when their neighborhood volcano erupted in 1968... the Fortunate indeed.

The massive Arenal volcano continues to rumble, and spit fire and rocks 40 years later, and constantly threatens to turn La Fortuna into a lava-paved parking lot. The folks there constantly live under the shadow of death, yet they go on with life – they work, play, marry, raise families.

A verse came to mind from Matthew 24:38: "For in the days before the flood, people were eating and drinking, marrying and giving in marriage, up to the day Noah entered the ark; and they knew nothing about what would happen until the flood came and took them all away. That is how it will be at the coming of the Son of Man."

While wandering the streets of La Fortuna, we visited a tiny sidewalk food stand, where a very friendly young man engaged us in conversation. He persuaded us that his father could make us a wonderful spicy burrito, if we could wait a few minutes. Everything smelled great.

Unfortunately, (La Unfortuna?) I was able to see into the kitchen. Unlike other places I had eaten there, it was absolutely filthy. I saw the cook wipe the chicken blood off his hands with a dirty rag, then proceed to lovingly manhandle all of the ingredients into my burrito, served with a smile.

I took the burrito in a sack, thanked them for their hospitality, and left. Even though I was very hungry, the burrito ended up in the first trashcan I found down the street.

Thinking Deeper:

We are all a bit like the cook in that little village. We go on with our lives in the shadow of sudden death and destruction, offering God gifts made with our filthy sin-stained hands. God in his mercy saw our wretched condition, and provided a way out. All we need to do is accept the perfect gift of Jesus – the bread of life made with his clean hands - and we are freed from the shadow of death. Jesus said in John 6:51 "I am the living bread that came down from heaven. If anyone eats of this bread, he will live forever. This bread is my flesh, which I will give for the life of the world."

That is the message of Easter.

Indeed, we who know it are "The Fortunate".

Driving: Miss Daisy

1994

At about the age of 14 months, my son began his love affair with the automobile. At our house, any unlocked car was subject to a thorough inspection, including turning on the radio (full blast), the flashers, wipers, defroster, etc. This provides mom or dad with a great early morning heart rate booster upon starting the vehicle, as well as a regular functional test of all accessories. Whenever it would get unusually quiet outside, I looked for the telltale little blonde head bobbing just above the dashboard in one of our cars that I could have sworn I remembered to lock.

Our son's frequent companion was our pygmy goat, Daisy. The goat served as his "dog", and both of them liked the arrangement. (Since she eats mainly weeds and water and requires no license or expensive dog food, I'm not going to break the news to them!) We even got her a doghouse to complete the illusion.

Imagine my surprise the day that I had heard from neither in a while, and upon inspection, found Caleb in the passenger seat of the pickup, doors closed, all accessories on, and the goat was driving! Both looked out the window at me like it was the most normal thing in the world. At our house, maybe it is... 20 years later he was still driving a pickup truck, found a pretty girl to marry him, and took his engagement pictures with the goats.

A Father's Love

1995

Like my father before me, I grew up in the warm, sunny South and spent a lot of time playing outside with no shoes on, as God must have originally intended. We live in a fallen world however, and one day when I was about 8 years old, somebody (probably me) carelessly left a board in the yard with a rusty nail poking up. Skipping along in front of my Dad, coming back from the garden, I stepped right on that nail and got a nasty puncture wound. Without a thought, Dad threw me down to the ground, grabbed my dirty little foot, and proceeded to suck the dirty blood out of the wound. He told me later that he did this so I would not get "lockjaw" from the rusty nail.

When Dad was a boy in the 1920's in Georgia, there was no such thing as a Tetanus shot, and wound sucking was apparently the first aid treatment of choice for rusty nail punctures! The whole affair was painful, and kind of gross, but from that day forward I always knew that my Dad truly loved me. He took care of my needs without even stopping to ponder what danger might come to him from the germs on my little foot – he just wanted the best for his boy. I would not have done the same for my best friend, not for a year's worth of allowance, but Dad did it for me without a thought.

Twenty-five years later, I stood barefoot in my own garden, with a barefoot boy of my own, watching my 82-year-old dad cultivate the garden with the little tractor. Dad continued cultivating with the garden tractor, verrry slowly because it was his first time.

Dad was no stranger to cultivation, however. He cultivated my mother's love during WWII, until in due time he "harvested" a wife and eventually 3 children. I seem to recall him cultivating the seat of my pants a couple of hundred times, until a crop of acceptable behavior was produced in me. He cultivated his own garden for 40 years, reaping gratitude and friendship from dozens of neighbors who ate his fresh produce. And in his later years, he cultivated the love and affection of 5 grandkids that loved his stories about the "old days".

Finally, the tractor work was done, and Dad ambled up to the house, shaking his head in dissatisfaction with his work. I told him the job looked fine, especially for his first time driving the tractor. He looked surprised, and said "Didn't I do that yesterday too?" His old memory was playing tricks on him again. Maybe he just remembered doing lots of cultivating in his life – he just never needed the tractor before.

Thinking Deeper:

I have told my son the story of the nail wound and how I experienced my father's love, saving me from sickness. More importantly, I have told him the story of how our Heavenly Father used 3 nail wounds to save his children from the sickness and death of sin. Fathers don't think about the sacrifice, they just think of how they love their children.

Daddy's Helper

1995

My son Caleb has always enjoyed "helping daddy". Before he could walk, he would sit in the stroller for hours and watch me work. (This was my idea of "watching the baby" while my wife was out. Robin's discovery of a pair of greasy pliers in the stroller one day required a creative explanation!)

When Caleb was about 18 months old, I was up on the porch roof making repairs. Imagine my surprise at seeing a blonde cowlick and then a big grin appear above the edge of the roof as Caleb climbed the ten-foot ladder alone! He was so anxious to come help daddy that he never even looked down. I was so terrified that I could not do anything but hold him tight on the roof for 10 minutes. (Worse yet, I had to go down and confess to the Official Safety Monitor what had transpired while I was "watching the baby".

Thinking Deeper:

I think boys are born wanting to help dad and be with dad, at least for a few golden years. There was a period of time that Caleb's "help" aggravated me. He would get in the way, hide tools, slow me down, and generally frustrate my need to finish my all-important projects. I got to where I would shoo him away when I was working on something. After reading up on Christian fatherhood skills, I was embarrassed to realize that building bonds with my son WAS the all-important project, and I was blowing my big opportunity with him. I gradually changed my mindset to realize that working on a project was just a vehicle to spend interactive time with my son, and it did not need to be finished perfectly, or in record time. After a few years, he actually was able to give me some real help – fetching tools, holding parts, etc., and we had forged a pleasant working relationship.

As he got older, Caleb partnered with me in a number of service and ministry activities, as well as lots of projects around home. He went out with me every few months to help serve communion in nursing homes. I think he brought a lot more cheer to the elderly than I did! He helped prepare the communion, and read or recited a Bible passage for each person we saw, in addition to just being a smiling kid in a place that needs a little more joy. I'm sure he would probably rather have been watching TV or playing, but we still had good experiences serving together. My hope and prayer is that this has built a life-long bond between us, and established in him the habit of serving others in Christ. Now *there's* a project worth finishing!

A Spicy Valentine's Day

1994

The big day was coming up. The advertisers had built up expectations, the ladies would be keeping score, and on February 14, us men had to come through! My research suggested that the key is not the amount spent, it is to show her that you are thinking fondly of her often. Advance planning is key. Rushing out at the last minute on the big day only proves to your love that you have not been thinking of her enough in the weeks before.

One year, after weeks of diligent fond thoughts about my wife (but no actual purchase action), I went out on my lunch hour on Feb 14 to a big classy spa to get my beloved a gift certificate. Unfortunately, there were 50 thoughtless, procrastinating scoundrels in line in front of me making their own last-minute purchases. Running short on time, I desperately thought of an alternate plan! I had seen a small, plain looking "relaxation spa" down the road that would surely be less crowded. I zipped into the parking lot, and entered the small spa.

Oddly, there was no receptionist, just a closed door off the waiting room. I knocked on the door, and in a few moments a very attractive, scantily clad foreign woman opened the door about 6 inches. Perplexed, I mumbled something about wanting to buy a gift certificate for my wife. With a look of disgust, she scornfully responded "We no do women here!" and slammed the door. Realizing my error, I quickly scanned the parking lot for witnesses and slinked away – back to the big spa to occupy the space I deserved, in line behind the other 50 guys. Fortunately, I was not picked up by the Vice Squad.

Thinking Deeper:

Our wives do not want to have to hint, remind or threaten us about Valentine's Day, Anniversaries, Birthdays. They want us to think about them often, and do the little things that show that we love them. Planning ahead shows thought. Picking out something that she really likes shows that you really know her. Phone calls and personal love notes go a lot farther than a big fancy card. Spending a lot of money is a poor substitute for your loving thoughts and actions.

Ephesians 5:23 says: "Husbands, love your wives just as Christ loved the church and gave himself up for her".

He Sacrificed So That We Could Be Free

1969

When I was a young boy, I was aware that my dad had some limitations that other dads did not. First, he was in his late fifties when I was in elementary school, about 20 years older than the other dads. He seemed pretty restrictive and old-fashioned as I grew up in the "hip" decades of the 60s and 70s. He also had problems with some burn scars on his legs. He could not run at all, which meant that we never played most sports together.

When we did go outside, to the swimming pool or the lake, he had to take a lot of precautions to protect his legs from the hot Texas sun. There was a great time-consuming ritual of unwrapping his legs and putting lotion on them, followed by a very slow cleaning and re-wrapping of the legs after swimming. It seemed like he could only swim with me for a few minutes at the price of an hour's worth of "leg work". When we were outdoors, even with long pants on, Dad had to be careful not to hit his shins on anything sharp, because he would bleed profusely. I remember being startled at the amount of blood that flowed just from hitting his shin on a rock. It seemed to me like a major injury, but he took it in stride.

One year, we had planned and saved for months to go to Disneyland in California, the trip of all trips for a kid in the 1960s! There was nothing to compare to Disneyland back then. As the day approached, I heard some murmuring about some type of ulcer that would not heal on Dad's leg. Then, one terrible day, my mom broke the news that we were going to cancel the trip because of Dad's leg – an ulceration that had been troublesome for many years simply would not stop bleeding, and he had to be on bed rest. I was crushed, angry, and pouted for days like the selfish little boy that I was.

As the years went by, I became less reliant on my dad for fun, and began to appreciate the fact that he was tough as nails. He never complained about his legs, and he had a very powerful upper body for a man his age, able to do 20 pull ups and climb a long rope hand-over-hand even at the age of 75. I also became aware that his leg injuries were a badge of honor from his service in World War II – a memento of a fiery plane crash that almost cost him his life. I took some pride in the fact that he was a veteran, and had sacrificed so that my generation could be free.

It took me until dad's military burial in 1997, when he was 83, to truly appreciate and weep for his wounds and his sacrifice. He walked the earth for 53 years with 3rd degree burn scars covering both legs, wounds that would not heal, and with crushed, fused bones in his ankle. He worked every day, married, raised 3 kids, and did his part in the church and the community, all without complaint. The 21-gun salute from the Marines on the day of his burial was the only recognition he ever received for his sacrifice. The memory of my childhood anger about the missed trip to Disneyland felt shameful to me.

Thinking Deeper:

During Easter 2004, walking out of the movie *"The Passion of the Christ"*, many of the same feelings surfaced. I grew up knowing about Jesus, his wounds, and his crucifixion. I recalled resenting Jesus at times for preventing me from visiting the "Disneyland of pleasures" that many of my high school and college friends seemed to live for. Seeing on the screen the horrors of what He endured, for me, without complaint, was more than I could stand to look at or talk about. I thank God that because of Jesus' sacrifice, and the fact that he bore my sin and punishment, I have been forgiven and will live forever with Him. I never want to take that sacrifice for granted again. I know that my Dad is with Jesus now, and I hope that they can somehow look down together and see that their boy has grown up a little.

The Geese

2005

Every year, about a month before Easter, a couple of Canadian geese come to stay at our pond for a while. They scout the area carefully, scare away any other waterfowl, and begin to build their nest on the corner of a small island. After a few days, mother goose is sitting on her nest of eggs, and daddy goose is out patrolling the pond and looking for food. We enjoy watching them every day for weeks while the eggs mature.

One year, I went out on the island Easter morning to find 8 little yellow-green fuzz balls all chirping as they followed mother goose in and out of the water for their first swimming lesson. They were just so darn cute; I wanted to get closer for a picture. Unfortunately, I had not cleared this with Goose Security Central, because both parents started hissing loudly and running at me with their 5-foot wings extended. Not wanting to start off Easter Sunday with a goose bite, I snapped the picture and ran.

I then watched an amazing thing. The mother somehow herded all 8 of the frightened little chicks one by one under her wings.

All 8 virtually disappeared under her protective wings. Only a few muffled chirps betrayed the fact that they were still there. After a minute, one adventurous little fellow popped his head out of the feathers for a look around, and eventually worked his way out of the protective covering of wings.

Thinking Deeper:

When Jesus was in Jerusalem just before his crucifixion, he said to the people "O Jerusalem, Jerusalem, you who kill the prophets and stone those sent to you, how often I have longed to gather your children together, as a hen gathers her chicks under her wings, but you were not willing." (Matthew 23:37)

That Easter morning, I got to see scripture come alive. The goose was willing to sacrifice herself to save her chicks, just as she was willing to spend her life to feed, nurture and protect them. The chicks just had to be willing to be gathered and protected. How often does Jesus call us to come to the safe place under his wings? Are we willing to go there, or do we insist on taking care of ourselves? Do we stay there and bask in the safe warmth, or do we pop back out when the danger is past? These are good things to ponder on Easter morning, as we think of the sacrifice of the One who gave all to save us.

Major Edward "Ned" Hodgson, USMCR, before his crash

A Man They Never Knew

1997

The funeral procession slowly wound around the low Georgia hills to Dad's burial site. Suddenly I saw them, and I was flooded with emotion: a dozen Marines in dress blues, polished, shined, and detailed to perfection, standing at attention.

They were there, on their day off, guarding the honor of a man they never knew. None of them were even born when he was pulled, more dead than alive, from the burning wreckage of an ill-fated night fighter training mission in 1942. Dad was raised in the segregated south, yet half the Marines were of a different hue. The preacher preached, the mourners mourned, and the silent sentinels stood still as stone.

Seven of the Marines crisply raised their rifles and fired; twice, thrice. They never knew that those 21 shots were Dad's only public recognition for steadfastly enduring the pain of his wounds for 55 years, as he fought the daily battles to live out a life of impeccable integrity as an officer, then a husband, father, citizen, and businessman.

Four more Marines reverently folded the flag of the country they loved and served. They gently tucked the 21 spent rifle shells into the folded flag. They didn't know that Dad had tucked in 8 children and grandchildren just as gently. The Commander stepped forward to present the flag to the family. He quietly spoke the feelings that reverberated in the still air: "With deep sympathy and thanks from a grateful nation for honest and faithful service." The mournful strains of Taps floated softly over the hill, conveying a deep sense of peace and finality.

The Marines slipped away in lockstep, as quietly and anonymously as they had come, to drive hundreds of miles back to their base. The memory of their gesture of honor and respect will remain.

They never knew Dad; they never knew his life of quiet heroism.

But they knew he had risked his life to defend their country.

They knew he was Lt. Col. E.M. Hodgson, USMC - a fellow Marine.

They saw that we loved him.

That was enough.

Semper Fidelis.

The Marine motto "semper fidelis" means "always faithful".

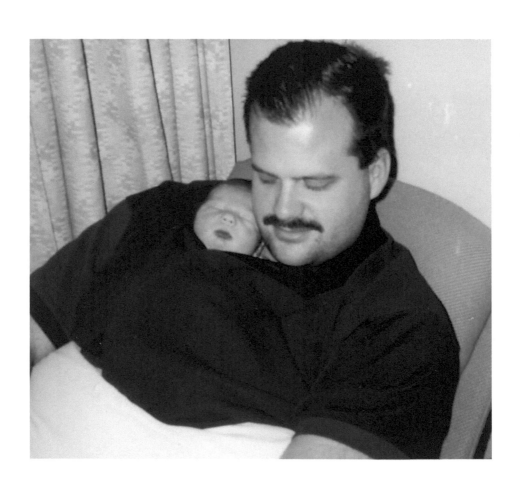

A "Baby Hog"

1993

My fatherhood experience started with a rude kick in the back. I was napping soundly one Sunday afternoon with my pregnant wife snuggled close behind me, when I was jolted awake by a sudden jab. "Hey! What was that for?" I said with some annoyance to my wife. I then fully realized for the first time that there was a 3rd person in bed with us, who apparently wanted my attention. Nothing has been the same since.

For the next few months, I would regularly have a fatherly chat with the little kicker in Robin's belly, getting a jump start on parenting by saying things like "daddy loves you", "mind your mother", and "clean your room" to help him get started on the right track. It was a wondrous thing to think that with God's help we had made a little life, and he was already interacting with us.

A few months later, when the doctor handed me a big, fine, baby boy I was instantly changed. I was overwhelmed with emotion thinking about things that we would do together, imagining him working side by side with me on our little farm. It is amazing the instantaneous love and affection that God gives you for your babies. I would have done anything for him, even died for him, right then – and we had just met!

Mom and baby were sleepy for a few days from the anesthesia, while I was exhausted from the strain of "going natural" during the whole birth process. For nap-time, which lasted pretty much all day for a few days, I stuffed little Caleb inside my shirt. He loved it in there, snug and warm, and would sleep contentedly for hours. Many a nurse was startled coming in and finding all of us asleep with two heads sticking out of my collar. It was really a great bonding time for us, even though I had to endure my wife accusing me of being a "baby hog".

For many years I read the bible and attended church, and I formed a vision in my mind of God as a protective, yet stern father. I assumed that what he wanted from me was obedience, and that if I misbehaved, I would suffer his disapproval. Intellectually, I knew that God had given us marriage and the family as a model of how He wanted us to relate to Him.

One day, coming home from a hard day at work, my son ran on his chubby little legs to greet me at the safety gate, beaming with a 2-tooth grin, reaching up to me with both arms and excitedly yelling "Da-Da!" to me over and over. As I scooped him into my arms, I finally realized what the heavenly Father must really want from his children. He even explained it in Romans 8:15: "For you did not receive a spirit that makes you a slave again to fear, but you received the Spirit of sonship, and by him we cry, "Abba, Father." – which is Aramaic for "daddy!"

I think I get the picture now.

Thirsty

1984

I get thirsty a lot, but I usually have a big mug of water nearby, so I drink without really thinking about it. Back in the 1980's, my college roommate Ronnie and I decided to take a hike into the Pecos Wilderness area in New Mexico just to get away from it all. We drove to the last small town on the map, filled up on gas, and then drove another 30 miles down a gravel road to the wilderness. We parked, strapped on our packs, and headed out for adventure.

Our topographical map indicated that there was a spring with a water well on top of the mountain we aimed to climb, so we only took a quart canteen of water each to keep our load light. The mountain trail was only maybe an inch long on the map, so we figured we would be at the top in no time! Unfortunately, that inch turned out to be like climbing the stairs up a 350-story building with 30 pounds on our backs. My canteen was empty in about a half hour, and we still had to climb all morning to get to the 10,000-foot rim of the tabletop mountain.

With screaming thighs and parched mouths, we began searching earnestly for the water well at the top. We walked a couple of miles before we found our "oasis" of spring water: a small rock well with no bucket, no pump, no rope, and just a puddle of questionable looking water about 6 feet down. Thirst being the mother of invention, I lowered Ronnie (the trusting fool!) head first into the well, as I held his ankles (what could go wrong?). He managed to fill up both canteens with what we would have to accept as "water".

A couple of hours later, we had built a fire, boiled the water and added iodine to kill the unfriendly microbes. We were each rewarded with a quart of very warm grape Kool-Aid flavored iodine water for our 8 hours of sweaty exertion. It was nasty, but it kept us from thinking we were going to die of thirst long enough to find a real stream on the backside of the mountain the next afternoon. (Health Note: apparently iodine causes certain bodily emissions to turn fluorescent green, which is harmless but rather startling!)

On the 3rd day, we made it back to the truck, and after a hasty drive to McDonald's, I slurped down the most delicious water I had ever experienced. In fact, for the next week, I could not pass a water fountain without getting a drink and marveling at how good it was.

I never knew how good water was until I experienced true thirst.

Thinking Deeper:

The people living in arid Israel in Jesus' day were probably thirsty a lot, and had to make do with a limited supply of warm, not very clean water. Jesus told them that he was the Living Water, and if they drank of Him, they would not thirst again! He also told them to hunger and thirst after righteousness. What powerful images for people living in that hot, dry land! Kind of makes you want a drink right now, doesn't it? I would venture to say that most of us modern Americans have really never been thirsty enough to understand.

I recommend the Living Water, no boiling or iodine tablets required.

Confessions of a Packrat

2002

In 2002, we moved for the first time in 10 years, and for the first time ever with kids. As we packed up to go, there was the inevitable whining and crying about each treasured item that would be given away or thrown away to lighten the move. (And that was just me! The kids adjusted pretty well.) For years, I gleefully accepted my friends' cast offs, because I thought I might use them later. Yes, the ugly truth is: I am a Packrat. As I packed, hauled, stored, unpacked, re-stored and searched for misplaced items, I began to ponder what God would have me learn from this rather unpleasant 2-week ordeal. Here are a few hard-learned lessons:

America is a land of excess – Matthew 6:21 "For where your treasure is, there your heart will be also."

We threw away more "stuff" than most families in the world own. We then called the Salvation Army truck and gave away twice that much. With all that done, it still took 3 movers 12 hours to move our remaining "good stuff". It is said that only Americans have Garage Sales. I assume that people in other countries have too little cash or too much good sense to buy things they do not need.

As an American dad, I must fight a constant battle for my family not to be overcome by materialism.

We need to do more to help the poor, especially the "working poor" - I John 3:17 "If anyone has material possessions and sees his brother in need but has no pity on him, how can the love of God be in him?" The guys who moved us worked really hard, on a hot day, for 12 hours. The moving company charged me over $1400, but then paid each of those guys less than a hundred bucks to feed their families. They gladly accepted some of our old furnishings as a gratuity, and planned to then give their own old furnishings to some less fortunate people in their neighborhood. Statistics show that the lower a person's income, the higher percentage of their income they tend to give to charity. Living in the more affluent part of town, it is easy to lose touch with real life, and real life is tough every day for a lot of people at the lower end of the earning scale.

Eventually, your "stuff" owns YOU, not the other way around - Matthew 6:19: "Do not store up for yourselves treasures on earth, where moth and rust destroy, and where thieves break in and steal". So many of the "treasures" I had stored away in the barn or the garage were damaged from moth, rust, water, mice, cobwebs, even raccoons. I spent an inordinate amount of time storing the stuff, then attempting to clean it up, only to end up giving it away or throwing it away. Better to have never gotten it in the first place, or at least to have given it away when I no longer needed it and freed myself from the clutter, thereby freeing up the time that the clutter then steals from me.

"Stuff" wastes your time that could be devoted to God. Matthew 19:21, Jesus said, "If you want to be perfect, go, sell your possessions and give to the poor, and you will have treasure in heaven. Then come, follow me."

I Corinthians 7:29-31 "What I mean, brothers, is that the time is short. From now on... Those who use the things of the world, [should live] as if not engrossed in them. For this world in its present form is passing away. "

Lesson Learned. I will now live the life of a "reformed" packrat; but please don't test me by calling to offer your cast-off treasures. I may not be fully recovered yet!

My First Rodeo

1981

There is an old saying in Texas, to let others know that **you** know what you are doing: "this ain't my first rodeo, you know". (Nobody ever tells the story of when it actually **was** their first rodeo.) When I was in college at Texas Tech in the 1980s, we had an annual intramural rodeo. My fraternity entered a team, and since I was the biggest guy, they nominated me to enter the "Steer Wrestling" event. Being a testosterone fueled 20-year-old, I naturally accepted immediately. In hindsight, I should have pondered the consequences of the fact that I had no idea how to wrestle a steer, or that the steer in question weighed in excess of 650 pounds, and had long horns to boot.

On the appointed night, I crawled into the starting gate or "chute" with my wrestling partner. He seemed a bit ill tempered as I gripped his three-foot horns securely and held on. I heard a horn blare loudly from somewhere over my head, the door to the chute flew open, and a cowboy hit the steer right in the rump roast with a 10,000-volt shock from an electric cattle prod. The immediate sensation was something like getting pulled out of the water by a ski boat – my body streamed back horizontally from my death grip on the horns.

About a half second later, as he skidded to a sudden stop, the laws of physics caused my body to sail over his head and land upside down in the dirt, while keeping my death grip on the horns. I suddenly found myself nose to nose with a very angry bovine. I briefly considered letting go of his horns, while he briefly considered stomping my head into the dirt. In desperation, I summoned all of my strength and turned his head like a steering wheel, dislocating my shoulder in the process. He fell on his side, and I sprinted like a rabbit for the safety of the side rails. Over the laughter of the crowd, I heard the announcer say: "A new school record! 4.7 seconds!" My record lasted for about 15 minutes, until somebody showed up who knew what he was doing. My dislocated shoulder lasted about 6 weeks.

Thinking Deeper:

I Corinthians 10:13 says: "No temptation has seized you except what is common to man. And God is faithful; he will not let you be tempted beyond what you can bear. But when you are tempted, he will also provide a way out so that you can stand up under it. "

Sometimes, we reach out and grab sin by the horns just because we want to. Frequently, that sin drags us to a frightening, dirty place where we do not wish to be. But God does not let us get our head completely stomped into the dirt; he gives us a way out of the situation. That way out may cause us some pain, but we can escape to live another day with God's help.

Mother's Day

2001

Sometime back in the 1960's, with my bare feet cool in the soft spring grass of Texas, my father took me a step closer to maturity. As we walked, I said: "Dad, whatcha gonna get mom for Mother's Day?" His profoundly logical response was: "What are YOU going to get her? She's not *my* mother you know." A light flashed on in my 8-year-old brain, suddenly grasping the increasing personal responsibilities of my age, and I got mom a gift from then on.

About 3 decades later, I was able to have an almost identical conversation with my own young son. He said "Oh! I get it!" and made his mom a small gift and card. For extra measure, I explained the logic to his 4-year-old sister, and she made a card too. Up until that year, I had always gotten cards and gifts on behalf of my kids to give to their mom, but now they had reached the age of responsibility, and freed me of a chore in the process.

Smug in my parenting success, I thought the big day went rather well. At the end of the day, however, I sensed some disappointment in my lovely wife. After some probing, I found out that she was hurt that I had not gotten her a card myself. An odd reaction, thought I. Dad's wisdom popped immediately into my mind, and I quipped: "Well, of course, you are not *my* mother!" (Marital Safety Tip: Don't try this at home.)

Well, let me just say that I now understand the true meaning of Mother's Day from a mother's perspective. It is a day to give honor and thanks to all the mothers in your life, not just your own mom. Personally honoring the mother of your own offspring as a great place to start.

Moms do a lot that it is hard for us men to really grasp. I have heard it said that to be a mother is to forever have part of your heart living outside your body. Mothers have a God-given ability to truly feel what their children feel. Mothers' ears are finely tuned machines. I was able to fall sound asleep with my babies wailing inches from my ear. My wife could wake up from a sound sleep at the sound of a pacifier dropping on the soft carpet in the next room, and know exactly what it was.

Even a mother's nose is especially sensitive, able to detect the faintest whiff of dirty diaper from across the room. I cannot count how many times I heard: "can't you *smell* that?!" It is remotely possible that dads intentionally mute their sense of smell so that they can avoid changing a dirty diaper and still look innocent, but I am not confessing. Many times, my wife has diagnosed illness, fatigue or lies just by looking my kids in the eye. We all know about mothers having eyes in the back of their heads. How do they do that?

I think that God designed women with these special abilities to allow them to be better mothers, and to make them uniquely qualified for their role in the family. Paul even uses the example of mothers' tenderness in 1st Thessalonians 2:7: "As apostles of Christ we could have been a burden to you, but we were gentle among you, like a mother caring for her little children."

Another Day in Paradise

1992

The house we moved into in 1992 was only beautiful in spots; it would take years for the reality to match the vision I had of it the day I first saw it and imagined the possibilities. (I envisioned; my wife cried.) Somehow my vision and salesmanship coupled with her blind devotion persuaded her, and we left our comfortable, average middle-class neighborhood to move just out of town to 5 acres with a 50-year-old house and barn.

There were many trials: the foundation cracks, the rewiring, the plumbing, the sheetrock dust *everywhere*, and the bold mice who would run across the living room right in front of us! Some days I felt like crying, and my wife had the vision (of our old middle-class neighborhood)! But then came spring. Glorious Spring! Daily little bulbs and flowers planted in years gone by surprised us by poking their little heads up. The Dogwoods bloomed in a spectacular blaze of pink and white all up and down our 500-foot drive. The sixty-foot trees surrounding the house enveloped us in a cool green canopy that the hottest days of summer didn't penetrate.

I mowed the field once, in sections, and it took a total of 10 hours. I then cleverly declared it a "meadow" instead of a "lawn", as the grass, clover and wildflowers were waist high within a month. A sweet smell from somewhere, (or maybe everywhere?) was always just outside the door. A hundred birds sang 4-part harmony in the trees all day, interrupted on occasion by the high-pitched chirp of a young one in need of a worm from mamma.

Our pygmy goat Daisy, grazed happily on the smorgasbord of plant life all around. Our miniature pig, Petunia, thought she was a goat too, and grazed alongside (blissfully unaware that pigs cannot metabolize protein out of grass!). Our bunny, Oreo, sat like a plaster statue in the same spot on the lawn all day, every day. No one knew why, but she seemed happy.

In the evening, as I headed into the house with an armload of fresh cut asparagus from the garden, I heard a strange noise. The deep bass grunts of a seemingly enormous animal headed my way through the waist deep grass. The grass parted at my feet, as Petunia emerged; only 8 inches tall, wanting a belly scratch from daddy. I happily obliged.

It is a marvelous thing to live closely connected to God's creation.

The Machete

1999

Something innate in a man makes him want to explore the wilderness and tame it. God sent Adam out to explore and subdue the earth, and several years ago, I purchased some acreage in the country and set out to do just that. It was completely overgrown with thorns and underbrush as well as mature trees.

On the weekends I would drag my family out there to 'explore and subdue". One fine fall day, with the family fully deployed into the woods, I pulled out my freshly sharpened machete to cut some underbrush. There is nothing like the effortless way a sharp blade cuts through the underbrush to make you feel like you are really the Master of your Domain.

Vines and saplings fell away before me, as I slashed like Conan the Barbarian through the woods. I found that with a loud yell and a mighty swing, I could cleave small saplings in a single stroke. I progressively tried bigger and bigger trees, until I came upon one that was almost 2 inches thick. Bracing myself for the extra heavy swing, I grabbed the tree firmly in my left hand and swung a mighty Conan-worthy stroke with my right. It sliced right through the tree like hot butter. Right through the tree and right through my pants and right through the skin to chop a notch in my left shinbone.

The nice thing about a really sharp blade is that it barely hurts when it cuts you. I did not really realize what I had done until I felt my boot filling up with something warm and wet. Trying to sound urgent but not alarming, I yelled across the field to my wife: "Honey... I need to go to the hospital... now". A veteran of the high-speed E.R. trips, she and the kids jumped in the 1979 Suburban and drove me the 20 minutes to the hospital. An interesting science factoid: you can tell how fast your heart is beating by noticing how often blood spurts out of a severed artery. Even a small one has a lot of blood in it, and you have to press really hard to make it stop.

At the hospital, I then learned a sociological lesson: if you are dirty and sweaty and wearing smelly blood-stained overalls, the ER nurses are not as nice to you. One yelled at me for bleeding on the furniture. I offered to stop bleeding if someone would just sew me up. The actual sewing took quite a while, since it also involved digging some tree particles out of my shinbone.

A saved the pant leg from that pair of overalls as a little memorial to my experience. I hung it with my tools with a little sign just below the bloody cut in the fabric that read: "Think".

They say that good judgment comes from experience, and experience comes from bad judgment

John F Hodgson

Pond Scum

2004

When the kids were little, we built a small lake to swim and fish in. The first year the water was crystal clear, and great to swim in all summer. The family and I had a blast playing together. The next summer, a most uninvited green and slimy intruder came to live in the pond. If you have spent any time in the country, you have seen it: pond scum. My little girl feared it and would scream if it floated near her. My wife sneered contemptuously at me for even being willing to get in the water with it. My son came up with excuses for not wanting to swim.

Ever the protective father, I started a major campaign against Mother Nature – I raked the scum out, I sprayed scum killer, I tried all the remedies the farm store recommended. A few weeks later and $200 poorer, I looked out over my beautiful… scum covered pond, a beaten man.

As the weather got hotter, the family became more willing to try to splash the scum out of the way just to get in and cool off. Scum terror began to diminish for the girls. My son began to experiment with the scum, and found it to be not too offensive. By September, the inevitable happened: the first Scum War.

Much to my kids' delight, the scum will wad up like a snowball and can be thrown a long way with a great "splat" effect on impact. Neighborhood kids joined in the fight. As the scum war intensified, the scum actually became harder to find – it takes a lot of scum to make a scum ball. Eventually, the pond was almost stripped clean, and the kids were sad because there was no more scum to play with. The following spring, the return of the scum was the cause of much rejoicing in the neighborhood. Over the course of only 12 months, we had gone from scum-fearers to scum-lovers, all without even being aware of the change.

Thinking Deeper:

Pond scum is really harmless, but the scum of this world – sin – is not. It is easy to get de-sensitized to sin, just like the pond scum, and eventually it becomes a source of enjoyment. It is my job as a dad to protect my kids from the dangerous and sinful things as long as I can. That first taste of beer or puff of a cigarette is repulsive to most kids, but it does not take long to get used to it and learn to enjoy it in excess. That first violent, gory movie is frightening, but after a few dozen the mind seeks out an even bloodier thrill. That first peek at pornography is startling, but it can quickly become an addiction.

This is why the Bible warns us in Romans 16:19 "…I want you to be wise about what is good, and innocent about what is evil." and in James 4:4: "…don't you know that friendship with the world is hatred toward God? Anyone who chooses to be a friend of the world becomes an enemy of God." I am going to do my protective duty and keep the scum away. I hope my kids will grow up and thank me for it later.

John F Hodgson

The Sacrifice Lamb

1999

People who lived in New Testament times had sheep and shepherds all around them. They ate lamb, drank sheep's milk, and wore wool clothing. They sacrificed a lamb every year at Passover, for the sins of their family. The parables Jesus told about sheep and shepherds had to have been abundantly clear to them. Sheep are totally dependent on their shepherd. Without his constant care, they would not survive.

One February day that had a record snowfall, one of my sheep decided to give birth. Not in the barn, mind you, but out in 19 inches of wet snow. I carried the wet, scrawny, shivering, and pitiful looking lambs back to the barn, where I spent hours with towels and a blow dryer, warming them enough to live. Nature took its course, and in a few days, I had a fine, healthy looking pair of lambs.

Eight weeks later, I found myself experiencing something else that most families experienced in Jerusalem 2000 years ago. It was Passover (Easter) weekend, and I had a buyer for one of the lambs. He planned to kill the lamb and serve it for Easter dinner, just as his family had done for generations in Greece, "the old country".

I was up at sunrise, getting prepared. My wife glared at me from under the covers as she heard me sharpening the knife, knowing what I was going to do to that cute little lamb. I was not looking forward to it, and wanted to finish the task before my kids were awake and curious. I had sent animals to the butcher before, but this was the first time I had done the deed myself. If you farm, you can't get too attached to your livestock, or soon you will have a hundred pets to feed.

I walked out into the early morning mist. I tied a rope around one of the lambs and led him away. My customer arrived, and we held the lamb quietly on the ground. The sharp knife did its work, and the lamb made not a sound. The bright red blood sent steam into the cool air. The little lamb I had held to my chest and warmed to life 2 months ago twitched one more time, and breathed his last. At dinner the next day, the lamb would fulfill his purpose for being born; but my heart was very heavy that day.

Thinking Deeper:

Nearly 2000 years ago, Jesus told the people of Jerusalem that He was the Lamb of God to be sacrificed for them. We sing songs about the lamb, and we sing songs about being washed in the blood. We read that Jesus was like an unblemished lamb, and silent before his executioners. The people of Jerusalem knew exactly what He meant.

Even though the lamb was born to die, it grieved my heart to see it; even more so because it died silently, innocently, without protest. I know how I felt as the blood of this little lamb ran past my boots. How must God have felt as the blood of His only Son ran down the rough wood of the cross, to redeem a people who did not even care for Him as much as a farmer cares for his livestock?

Jesus is the shepherd, without whom we would surely die. But he is also the Sacrifice Lamb, without whom we cannot truly live

A Real Pig

1981

"Don't make a pig of yourself!" You might have heard this (like I did) from your mother a time or two in your teenage years as you shoveled down a heaping plate of food at the Thanksgiving table. I never experienced being "full" until I was about 18, and the concept of not eating when there was food left was a foreign one. The Bible has a lot to say about pigs and gluttons, and paints a vivid picture for us by their example.

Why does the pig get such a bad rap? My family had a pet pig – Zeke - who was like a member of the family. Being housebroken, he was free to open the screen door with his nose and come on in. He bathed daily in a swimming pool I built for him, and stayed as clean as any dog. He seemed to have an almost human intelligence to understand what we were saying to him, and could learn a variety of dog tricks – fetch, lie down, sit up, beg, etc. He could chew gum, and knew not to swallow it (he had minty-fresh breath!). Zeke drank milk from a glass without spilling any. He would even stick his snout under water and blow bubbles on command! So did he learn these tricks just to please us, his masters? No. He learned them to please his real master – his gluttonous appetite. He would do anything for food. Never did we see him do a single trick for "free" – there was always a promised treat.

In one shameful event during Zeke's piggy adolescence, I took him with me to a party. Everyone enjoyed feeding him popcorn, chips, peanuts and other snacks. Somebody thought it would be funny to give him a beer, which Zeke sucked right out of the bottle to the delight of the crowd. He lapped spilled beer off the floor. Eventually, he was sprawled on the floor, too full and drunk to walk, and making feeble piggy grunts for more beer and peanuts. He was also too drunk to make it to the Piggy-Port-O-Potty, and all that rich food had to go somewhere. Zeke had worn out his welcome, and we left in shame. My mother was pretty angry that I brought home a hung-over, incontinent pig for her to nurse back to health. Proverbs 28:7 confirms my experience: "He who keeps the law is a discerning son, but a companion of gluttons disgraces his father." I pledged not to take Zeke to any more parties.

After a few years' ample food, Zeke started getting a little too big to handle. He was supposed to be a miniature pig, but he got to be about 350 lbs. We tried to put him on a piggy diet, but he began to hate us for it. He got grumpy and ill tempered. He snapped at the hand that fed him, demanding more. He bit one of the smaller kids. One time he found a bag of feed that had broken open and tried to eat the whole thing, and his belly swelled up so much that he could not get up.

As Zeke reached piggy adulthood, he also began to grow sharp tusks. Once my mother was trying to give him some affection, and he cut her open with a careless toss of his head, requiring mom to get stitches. The Bible confirms this pig behavior in Matthew 7:6: "…do not throw your pearls to pigs. If you do, they may trample them under their feet, and then turn and tear you to pieces."

The second time Zeke sent Mom to the hospital for stitches, Dad grimly determined what must be done. He hired a "hit man". On the appointed day, as Zeke greedily slurped down his final meal of beer and peanuts, a bullet ended his short, gluttonous life. A passage from Proverbs 23 came to mind: "When you sit to dine with a ruler, note well what is before you, and put a knife to your throat if you are given to gluttony."

Thanks for the lesson Zeke.

My Little Valentine

2005

A friend of mine in Texas sat up late one night, just quietly watching his daughter sleep. Tears streamed down his face, and he was deeply troubled. His wife found him in this state and asked what was troubling him so. He said, "Can't you see? My little girl has met a boy, and tomorrow she is getting married and leaving me forever, and I am heartbroken!" His wife just shook her head and said: "Come to bed Walt, she is only 3 days old."

As my baby girl began to notice boys, I realized the years were passing too quickly. I joked about not letting her date until she is 30, and then she would only be allowed to see Seminary graduates. I made sure her older brother was trained to punch any of his friends that might inquire about going out with his little sister. I threatened to sit on the porch in my dirty overalls, holding my shotgun and sharpening my knife to greet any boy that should have the nerve to come calling. I wanted to put a sign at the end of the driveway that says: "If you can read this sign, you are within shooting range". Somehow, I aimed to protect her heart until a Godly young man should come along that loves her as much as I do.

I knew that I could only keep the boys away for so long, so my protection plan for her heart was to set such a high standard that she would not be interested in any boy who did not treat her right. I wanted her to know what it is like to be loved for her inner beauty, for her heart, and not just for outward appearance. I wanted her to know what it is like to be cherished and treated with love and respect rather than selfishness. I wanted her to know that I would gladly lay my life down to protect her. Above all, I did not want some boy who acted like I did as a teenager to come within 10 feet of her!

Thinking Deeper:

This experience of loving and protecting my daughter really helped me understand the Bible better. The scripture is full of references to God treating his people like a treasured daughter, pleading with them not to give their love to foreign gods. He has a groom of his own choosing for the big wedding – Jesus. In Revelation 21:2 we get a picture of the future event: "I saw the Holy City, the new Jerusalem, coming down out of heaven from God, prepared as a bride beautifully dressed for her husband"

John F Hodgson

(un) Easy Rider

1981

My 2nd year at college, I moved too far off campus to ride my bicycle to class. Parking the car was a hassle and a long walk. Naturally, this required me to buy a motorcycle.

A search of the newspaper ads and two hundred bucks later, I had a worn-out Honda 125 with a seat covered in blue jean material. Not much to look at, not too fast, but it was mine. I got it home and started learning to ride in the field behind my trailer house.

Balance was a little tricky – I was probably too tall for the bike, and my weight made the suspension bottom out, but I got the hang of it in the field. Dressed safely in flip flops, gym shorts, sunglasses and a smile, I ventured onto some of the trailer park's paved roads. Some tiny signal in the frontal lobe of my brain suggested to me that I was going too fast as I approached a patch of gravel in the road. I braked.

The brakes worked great, and I validated Newton's 1st law of physics. The bike stopped, and since my body was still in motion, it remained in motion and I came over the handlebars, pausing only to break a small bone in each bare foot on the engine block on the way over. Again, my frontal lobe pleaded with me, this time to spare my face. I put my hands out, saved the face, but lost the skin off both palms and one shoulder. A bit shaky, I got back on and rode slowly to the Quickie Mart for some alcohol and bandages, paying the horrified clerk with my shaky bleeding hands.

I soaked in the bathtub for a while to try to get the imbedded tar and gravel out of my skin. After getting as cleaned us as practical, I ventured over to see my neighbor Mike with a pair of scissors. Oddly, Mike balked when I asked him to cut off my palm flaps, each the size of a small thin pancake. For some reason, I could not bring myself to do it. He caught them on a paper plate; I can still remember the plopping sound.

Back in the trailer, I did an amateurish bandage job on the palms and shoulder. It didn't really matter, because blood kept soaking through and I had to change them pretty often. I sat and pondered my new awareness of every nerve ending in my palms, feet and shoulder.

Luckily, my roommate Phil came home with a solid idea: "If you drink enough, you won't be able to feel your hands." Simple, yet brilliant! Out of sympathy he joined me, and sure enough, by about 9:30 PM at the local bar, my pain was gone! Dr. Phil was a genius… until morning... Oh, how I cursed Phil in the morning. A hangover did NOT make my feet and hands and shoulder feel better, but the pounding of my head was somewhat distracting.

I went on to own a couple of larger bikes for about 10 years and never had another accident, having learned a valuable lesson that day. Scientists tell us that the frontal lobes (where risk is evaluated) are not fully developed in males until about age 30. The challenge is to live that long.

Ecclesiastes 7:17 - Do not be overwicked, and do not be a fool— why die before your time?

Deer Safety

2005

There are many dangers in our world today – traffic accidents, shootings, terrorism, hurricanes – and yet there is still one place that has proven to be absolutely safe. That place of absolute safety is the area directly around my tree stand during deer season. No deer has ever been injured there, much less killed. I sit in my tree, concealed by my high-tech camouflage clothing and deer scent, searching with binoculars and a high-powered rifle scope, and yet time and again the deer escape completely unscathed. Twice I have had large deer close enough that I could have dropped my rifle on their heads to stun them, and yet I was too slow to get a shot off. Some 3000 Kentucky deer kill themselves by jumping in front of cars every year. I am considering skipping the camo clothing next year, and just dressing up as a Toyota.

Some of the first Christians in America had a great Feast of Thanksgiving in the Autumn of 1621. They had miraculously survived their first winter, planted crops, and reaped a harvest that year. The local Wampanoag Indians brought them 5 deer as a part of the feast, and for that and the other food they were truly thankful to God! As I eat my Kroger turkey this year, I will thank God that I am not dependent on my hunting skills to feed myself and my family for the winter! Thanks to my neighbor Todd, I did eat deer all last winter, but my only contribution was to help drag it out of the woods. Apparently, the conditions near his tree stand are much more dangerous than near mine.

Either that, or the deer are so preoccupied laughing at my feeble hunting attempts that they are off guard when they wander past Todd's tree.

One part of hunting that has been great is spending time with my son. Hunting is a very elemental experience that has been shared between fathers and sons for thousands of years. My dad only took me bird hunting once in my life, but I still remember the day, the thrill and danger of handling a gun, and the excitement of the hunt. Proverbs 4:1 says: "Listen, my sons, to a father's instruction; pay attention and gain understanding." That was a great opportunity for me to learn gun safety and sportsmanship from my dad.

Thinking Deeper:

When you climb up in a slippery tree stand before dawn, with a gun and a bunch of gear, it is a little scary. It is a big challenge to try to be still and quiet while the critters in the woods around you wake up. Every deer-like sound in the dark woods makes our hearts quicken, and we look wide eyed at each other in anticipation of what might be coming towards us. It is great to share that experience with my son – a little cold, a little scared and excited, but together out in God's wild world.

There is an old saying that a picture is worth a thousand words. Well, for a couple of young boys hunting with their dads, every deer that is seen is worth at least 1000 words in the truck on they way home. So is reliving the story about getting the truck stuck in the mud and walking the 3 miles to town, and remembering how fabulous those greasy burgers and fries tasted on a very empty stomach. One of my "thanks" at Thanksgiving is for the chance to enjoy God's creation with my son and our good friends and make some great memories together.

John F Hodgson

The Dolphin in My Shower

1998

He's a curious thing,

the Dolphin in my shower.

He cannot talk, or even sing –

but he has a special power!

The bathroom looks a bit unkempt,

with him lounging in my bath;

He even tripped me once,

while lying in my path!

But I do not kick him out,

for one very special reason:

With him my Caroline bathes with glee

– but only for a season.

As time slips by so quickly,

my heart will treasure up this hour;

For a sad day it will be,

when there's no Dolphin in my shower.

Log Cabin Christmas

1994

My 7th Christmas in 1967 was a memorable one. My parents were tired of the hustle and hassle of an increasingly commercialized Christmas, and somehow, they snookered me and my older brother and sister into giving up our normal gifts in exchange for a week in a cabin in the Colorado Rocky Mountains. We arrived to find a small cabin 9000 feet up in the pine forest with no heat, no running water, no TV, no entertainment nearby, no kids my own age to play with, and of course no big Christmas gifts. It turned out to be the best Christmas holiday week of my life.

My father was partially disabled from WWII, and not a skilled woodsman, but he managed to get a roaring fire going in the fireplace to defrost the cabin. I helped him carry buckets of water from the icy creek a few times a day so that we could flush the toilet. We trudged through knee-deep snow deep into the forest and found a perfect 8-foot Christmas tree to cut and drag back to the cabin. We spent an evening around the dining table making our own ornaments out of colored paper and popcorn and thread, and no tree ever looked better to me when we were done.

The cabin consisted of one large room with several beds, so I had to bunk with my teenage sister. She built a defensive wall of pillows between us, since I was well known as a "thrasher" when I slept. Dad would load up the fire every night with wood, and pile up the ashes to keep the heat in while we slept. It was an absolutely marvelous feeling of security having my whole family clustered together against the cold, with not a sound in the world but the fire crackling and my dad snoring. Mom found the snoring to be less than marvelous, but I didn't mind.

We spent our days trying to slide down the hill on some contraption that was a cross between a wooden ski and a scooter. It was a very efficient way to cram wet snow at high velocity into every imaginable crevice and fold of clothing. The era before waterproof ski clothes made it mandatory to spend a couple of hours drying out and talking in front of the fire every afternoon.

Christmas Eve was especially memorable. Our family was not very spiritual at that time, but sitting around the Christmas tree by firelight, with snow softly falling in the forest all around us set a perfect mood. Mom read the Christmas story out of Luke: "Today in the town of David a Savior has been born to you; he is Christ the Lord….", and we all sang a few carols. It truly was a silent night, a holy night. I imagined the baby Jesus huddled close by his loving parents against the cold night in his rough surroundings, and felt that all was right with my world.

Following Jesus' example, we all slept in Heavenly Peace.

Modern American Gothic?

Thanks for Reading!
The adventures will continue